The WIZARD of Oz™

THE MAKING OF A MASTERPIECE

by Randy Roberts

STERLING INNOVATION
New York

STERLING INNOVATION
New York

An Imprint of Sterling Publishing
387 Park Avenue South
New York, NY 10016

This 2013 edition published by Sterling Publishing Co., Inc., by arrangement
with becker&mayer! Books, Bellevue, Washington. www.beckermayer.com

Editor: Dana Youlin
Designer: Sarah Baynes
Image Researcher: Emily Zach
Production Coordinator: Jennifer Marx
Product Developer: Peter Schumacher
Illustrators: Greg Cook and Ryan Hobson

ISBN 978-1-4351-4840-6

This book is part of *The Wizard of Oz Paint-by-Number Kit*
and is not to be sold separately.

For information about custom orders, special sales, and premium
and corporate purchases, please contact Sterling Special Sales at
800-805-5489 or specialsales@sterlingpublishing.com

Manufactured in China

www.sterlingpublishing.com

Unless otherwise noted, all images are courtesy of Warner Bros. Entertainment Inc.
Image Credits: Page 6: The Wonderful Wizard of Oz, 1900 title page © William Wallace Denslow/
Wikimedia Commons. Page 7: The Wizard of Oz poster insert © Metro-Goldwyn-Mayer
(Cinemasterpieces)/Wikimedia Commons. Page 8: Wizard of Oz cast promotional image ©
NBC Television Network/Wikimedia Commons. Page 12: Judy Garland and Terry promotional
image © NBC Television Network/Wikimedia Commons. Page 15: Judy Garland and Margaret
Hamilton promotional image © NBC Television Network/Wikimedia Commons.

CONTENTS

PAINT-BY-NUMBER
INSTRUCTIONS

To create a *Wizard of Oz*–inspired masterpiece, simply match the numbers on the canvas to the corresponding paints. When you see multiple numbers listed, mix equal parts of each paint listed to create new colors. For example, 3/7 is equal parts paint 3 and paint 7, and 5/5/6 is two parts paint 5 and one part paint 6.

SUPPLIES:

- Cup of water for cleaning your brush
- Paper towels for blotting and brush cleaning
- Toothpicks for stirring paint
- Plastic wrap or piece of aluminum foil for paint mixing
- Newspaper or cloth to protect work surface

TIPS AND TECHNIQUES:

- Before beginning, refer to the color key for each canvas to see how many paint colors are needed and which colors will need to be mixed.
- To open paint pots, press the plastic teeth *toward* one another.
- Stir paint with toothpicks before getting started for best results.
- Smaller areas should be painted first, then move on to larger areas.
- For best results, paint areas that are a single number first, then begin color mixing.
- When mixing colors, start by mixing a small amount of paint to avoid having paint leftover.
- Match mixed paint to the color key given for each canvas before applying.
- Let paint dry completely before applying a second coat, if needed.
- Change your brush-cleaning water frequently to keep paint colors pure.
- Clean brush with soap and water after use.
- Be sure to close pots completely to avoid the paint drying out when not in use.

OVER THE RAINBOW

The JOURNEY *to the* SCREEN

In the seventy-five years since its premiere in 1939, *The Wizard of Oz* has become a touchstone in American and world popular culture in a way none of the other celebrated films of the year—including *Gone With the Wind*—have. The mere mention of the Yellow Brick Road and the Ruby Slippers stirs memories from childhood, and the phrase "We're not in Kansas anymore," suggests that a person has stepped into a different life. For more than a generation before the film, L. Frank Baum's *The Wizard of Oz* (1900) was a popular children's novel; but since 1939, the film has eclipsed the book.

Baum's story had been around before Hollywood was Hollywood. Why did it take so long for one of the moguls to turn it into a movie?

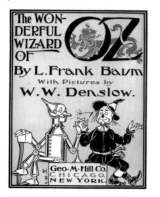

PUBLISHED IN 1900, *THE WONDERFUL WIZARD OF OZ* WAS A MUCH BELOVED CHILDREN'S STORY A GENERATION BEFORE MGM TRANSFORMED IT INTO A TECHNICOLOR MOVIE.

Part of the answer lies in the popular Hollywood truism that adults did not want to watch children's fantasy stories. That idea changed during the 1937 Christmas season when Walt Disney's *Snow White and the Seven Dwarfs* premiered. Within a year the film had grossed more than $4 million, a huge amount in those days, making it the top moneymaker for 1938. If Disney could make millions with a children's fairy tale, the Metro-Goldwyn-Mayer (MGM) studio heads could make more.

Success has many parents, but failure is an orphan: In no town is that more true than Hollywood, where ignoring truth and creating legends is what people do. This makes it difficult to get to the bottom of any story. We know, for example, that MGM chief Louis B. Mayer gave the order to purchase the rights to Baum's *The Wizard of Oz* for $75,000 at about the mid-point of the spectacular 1938 run of *Snow White and the Seven Dwarfs*. We don't know who convinced Mayer to make the purchase. Mervyn LeRoy, who became the producer of the film, claimed he did it. Arthur Freed, LeRoy's assistant on the film, said Mayer made the buy on his advice. Either way, the final purchase was completed on

June 3, 1938, and Mayer gave the property to LeRoy to produce. It was budgeted at more than $2 million, and for accounting purposes listed on the books as Production #1060. It was slated to be one of forty-one movies MGM released in 1939.

LeRoy was a product of vaudeville and the silent era in Hollywood, where he worked his way up from wardrobe assistant and bit actor to writer and gagman, and finally to director and producer. By 1938 he was a $6,000-a-week producer at MGM, which was widely regarded as the Tiffany of studios. Unlike today, where directors put their individual stamps on films, in the Studio Era, producers dominated the moviemaking industry. They oversaw everything from script development, casting, and choice

INITIALLY MGM'S *THE WIZARD OF OZ* WASN'T CARRIED BY A STAR. WHEN IT WAS RELEASED IN 1939 NEITHER JUDY GARLAND NOR THE OTHER MEMBERS OF THE CAST WERE HOUSEHOLD NAMES.

THE TIN WOODMAN, DOROTHY, THE SCARECROW, AND THE
COWARDLY LION FINALLY MEET THE WONDERFUL WIZARD.

of directors to key decisions concerning how the film was photographed,
edited, packaged, and sold. Producers fell just below studio moguls in
the Hollywood pecking order. The production process was their world,
and everyone in that world did as they were told. With such directing
credits as *Little Caesar* (1930), *I Am a Fugitive from a Chain Gang* (1932),
Gold Diggers of 1933 (1933), and *Anthony Adverse* (1936), Mervyn LeRoy
was a reliable veteran of the industry.

Not only did LeRoy know filmmaking, he had a deep connection with the themes of *The Wizard of Oz*. "Mr. Mayer bought the book for *me*," he said. "I wanted to make a movie out of *The Wizard of Oz* from the time I was a kid." LeRoy's childhood paralleled Dorothy's in many ways. When he was five his parents divorced, and when he was six his father's small department store was destroyed in the San Francisco earthquake. The combination of divorce and disaster subjected him to emotional and physical trauma, and—like Dorothy, an orphan—he must have felt at the mercy of an unsettled changing world. For LeRoy, life in Hollywood must have seemed as glittering and magical as Dorothy's time in the Emerald City.

WHEN DOROTHY ARRIVES IN MUNCHKINLAND, THE SHIFT FROM DRAB BLACK-AND-WHITE TO BRILLIANT TECHNICOLOR STILL SHOCKS THE SENSES.

DOROTHY

JUDY GARLAND'S STAR ASCENDS

It is not an exaggeration to say Judy Garland made *The Wizard of Oz*, and *The Wizard of Oz* made Judy Garland. It is possible to pinpoint the exact scene when *The Wizard of Oz* becomes a classic film. It is early in the movie—well before Dorothy's monochromatic "real" world jumps into her Technicolor "dream" world. She is an unhappy, misunderstood child. Miss Gulch plans to "destroy" Toto, and Auntie Em and Uncle Henry fail to understand the depth of Dorothy's anguish. Dorothy walks across a barnyard, talking to Toto, wondering if somewhere there's "a place where there isn't any trouble." She's sure there is. "It's not a place you can get to by a boat … or a train," she tells Toto. "It's a place far, far away … behind the moon, beyond the rain…." And then it happens.

SEVERAL EXECUTIVES AT MGM FELT THAT JUDY GARLAND WAS TOO UNATTRACTIVE TO PLAY DOROTHY. THEY WERE ALL TERRIBLY WRONG.

Judy Garland stops talking and begins to sing "Somewhere Over the Rainbow."

A moment before she begins to sing, Judy Garland is a plump, not particularly attractive (at least by MGM standards) girl in a high-waisted, blue-and-white-checked gingham dress. But the act of singing transforms her—she becomes a beautiful girl that the audience cares about. She absolutely sells the song. Her voice wobbles on the edge of breaking and her saucer-like eyes well with tears. It's a perfect match of song and performer.

The idea of a place "where there isn't any trouble" struck a sensitive chord with audiences in 1939. That year, while America was in the last painful gasp of the Great Depression, World War II began in Europe. But the idea touched closer to home for Judy Garland. She was born Frances Ethel Gumm in 1922 to vaudevillian parents, and show business was always part of her life. She appeared on stage for the first time when she was two-and-a-half, joining her older sisters Mary Jane and Dorothy to sing the chorus of "Jingle Bells." By the time Frances was six, the Gumm Sisters had become a song-and-dance act. They toured on the vaudeville circuit, made several film appearances, and even changed the name of the act to the Garland Sisters. In 1935 the newly renamed Judy Garland came to the attention of Louis B. Mayer and signed a contract with MGM. On the surface, at least, her life seemed the stuff of light romance.

But it wasn't. Hundreds of girls signed studio contracts and went through stressful years of singing, dancing, and acting lessons. Most were

A CYCLONE SWEEPING TOWARD DOROTHY TO FURTHER SHAKE UP HER WORLD.

dropped in a year or two when their contracts expired. Very few became successful actresses, and only a fraction of those became stars. Judy's chances did not look good. To begin with, she was overweight, had bad teeth, and was rather plain. Compared to some of the other young contract players at MGM in the late 1930s and early 1940s—including such future stars as Ava Gardner, Hedy Lamarr, Ann Rutherford, June Allyson, Lana Turner, and Elizabeth Taylor—Judy looked like the ugly duckling trailing behind a flock of graceful swans. Mayer referred to her as his "little hunchback," and other executives and wardrobe people openly discussed her flaws in front of her.

EVIL AND INNOCENCE—THE WICKED WITCH OF THE WEST AND
DOROTHY. ONLY ONE COULD SURVIVE.

"FOLLOW THE YELLOW BRICK ROAD." AND WITH THAT SIMPLE
DIRECTION DOROTHY WAS OFF TO SEE THE WIZARD.

But when she sang her flaws vanished. Her perfect contralto voice
and trembling, emotional range constantly saved her when studio executives debated her future. MGM cast her in a few singing cameo roles,
and she excelled. She also played a convincing girl-next-door opposite
Mickey Rooney. But at the beginning of 1938 she was still far from being
a star, and many questioned the wisdom of hitching her name to the
high-budgeted *Wizard of Oz*.

Several MGM executives, including Mayer and Nicholas Schenck, president of Loew's, MGM's parent company, wanted 20th Century-Fox's Shirley Temple to play Dorothy. Between 1935 and 1938 Temple was America's "little sweetheart," consistently topping all other performers at the box office. Furthermore, she was six years younger than Garland, and therefore much closer to the age of Dorothy Gale in Baum's novel. But other influential MGM executives favored Garland, who not only sang far better than Temple but also came much cheaper since she was an MGM employee. Assistant producer Freed and MGM musical arranger Roger Edens were strongly behind Garland. LeRoy later also claimed that she was his choice. "I always wanted Judy Garland," he told an interviewer. "On account of her voice. On account of her personality… I insisted we had to make a test of her, and she was sensational. I fixed all her teeth in front. She had big wide spaces. That was the first thing I did with Judy Garland."

Perhaps the combined efforts of Freed, Edens, and LeRoy carried the day. Or, more likely, Darryl Zanuck at Fox simply refused to loan Temple to MGM. Whatever the truth, Judy Garland got the part. Immediately the MGM publicity machine went to work, making sure that Judy—in person and onscreen—was showcased as an ingénue before the American public. MGM sent her on tour. They gave her the lead billing on another film. They labored to make her a star.

Her voice took care of the rest. Gingham dress from Kansas, Ruby Slippers from Munchkinland, and a voice to make you cry. Judy Garland wasn't in Kansas anymore.

THE RUBY SLIPPERS

The WORLD'S MOST FAMOUS PAIR of SHOES

They appeared suddenly and inexplicably on page 25, shot 114 of screenwriter Noel Langley's fourth revision of his script of *The Wizard of Oz*, the one he labeled "DO NOT MAKE ANY CHANGES." Langley wrote: "The Ruby shoes appear on Dorothy's feet, glittering and sparkling in the sun."

Ruby! Where did the inspired idea and the glorious color come from? They didn't come from L. Frank Baum's novel. He's quite explicit about the shoes. When the Good Witch of the North tells Dorothy that she—or at least her house—has killed the Wicked Witch of the East, Dorothy replies, "I have not killed anything." But then she looks at her house, and there, "just under the corner of the great beam the house rested on, two feet were sticking out, shod in silver shoes with pointed toes."

Langley, a tall, young writer at MGM, had never been quite sure about what to do with the magical shoes. He wrote them out of his first script, then brought them back in the second script, but their purpose was ill defined. By the "DO NOT MAKE ANY CHANGES" script they had become ruby and truly magical. They, after all, eventually transport Dorothy back to Kansas, a feat that the Wizard never had the power to achieve.

In an iconic film the Ruby Slippers are the most familiar and mentioned touchstone. Gilbert Adrian, MGM's chief costume designer, supervised the construction of the slippers. One person who recalled the wardrobe process said at first they tried coating different sorts of shoes

THEY WERE SILVER SLIPPERS IN L. FRANK BAUM'S NOVEL. BUT FOR SEVERAL GENERATIONS OF MOVIE-GOERS THEY WILL ALWAYS BE THE RUBY SLIPPERS.

"with a kind of shiny patent-leather paint." But none looked right, so they scrapped the paint idea. Next they tried several different slipper designs, from a heavily jeweled Arabian pair to more simple ones, and experimented with different types of beads. Finally, they attached sequins to organza and utilized the fabric in the construction of the shoes. They used darker red sequins to give the shoes their Technicolor ruby look, and after examining the work, Adrian added the butterfly-shaped red leather bows. Altogether, the shoemakers made six or seven pairs.

It worked perfectly, but the shoes were difficult for the cameraman to shoot. The sequins on the Ruby Slippers reflected light and ruined several takes. (The Tin Man's, costume did the same thing.) Technicolor photographer Harold Rosson remembered, "We had to avoid any light shining on them which would project the reflection into the camera." But as in the case of the shoes' construction, the cameraman's precautions were a small price to pay for the fabulous results. The shot of the deep ruby slippers, framed by Dorothy's sky-blue bobby socks and sparkling like precious jewels, was dazzling. It is impossible to imagine Dorothy wearing clunky silver footwear or patent-leather pumps.

But the construction and filming of the shoes did not explain why Langley and MGM decided on ruby rather than silver. The answer, unfortunately, is rather mundane. Margaret Hamilton, the Wicked Witch of the West and Dorothy's nemesis in the film, once asked producer Mervyn LeRoy why he didn't stick with Baum's choice of silver. Without hesitation, LeRoy said that in Technicolor red stood out better than silver against the Yellow Brick Road. It was all about pop—and how the ruby slippers did pop!

After *The Wizard of Oz* premiered and moved on to the screens of America and the world, the actual ruby slippers Judy Garland wore during production were forgotten. But early in 1970 a pair turned up in a bin in the basement of MGM's Wardrobe Department, wrapped in a Turkish towel. It was a sensational find, a relic of the Hollywood Studio System in its heyday.

At an auction of MGM memorabilia, the shoes brought $15,000, the highest amount for any item. Since then, other pairs have turned up, and the value of all have skyrocketed. In 1988 a pair sold for $150,000; in 2000 another pair went for $666,000; and today experts estimate a pair might go for two to three million dollars. After all, nothing spells classic Hollywood like the Ruby Slippers.

Different pairs of the slippers played special roles in the making of *The Wizard of Oz*. It is believed that Judy Garland used one pair during most of the production. This pair is now on display at the Smithsonian. Another pair was used for the close-ups in the movie, especially the shot when the shoes first appear on Dorothy's feet. This pair has scuffs that indicate they might also have been used for the shot when Dorothy clicks her heels to return to Kansas. Another pair was probably made for Garland's stunt double. The lining in the shoes indicates "Double," not "Judy Garland." Although most pairs are size 5, several are size 6 and 6½. They may have been used for photo shoots and publicity, or worn

THE WICKED WITCH CAN REACH, BUT SHE CAN'T TOUCH. THE RUBY SLIPPERS BELONG TO DOROTHY.

by Garland during afternoon work. Swollen feet led her to request a pair a half size larger.

Curators at the Smithsonian claim the Ruby Slippers are among the museum's most popular artifacts. Why? It might be because they are such a visible link to the Golden Age of Hollywood. They represent universal themes—the transition between innocence and experience, the fragile balance between loss and hope, the deep longing for adventure, and the desperate need for the safety of a home. Dorothy dreams about a place "over the rainbow," but she knows "there's no place like home."

THE GOOD, THE BAD, AND THE JUST PLAIN WICKED

The WITCHES of the MARVELOUS LAND OF OZ

When the winds of the cyclone died down and Dorothy's house stopped moving, L. Frank Baum told his readers, "She sprang from her bed and with Toto at her heels ran and opened the door. The little girl gave a cry of amazement and looked about her, her eyes growing bigger and bigger at the wonderful sights she saw. The cyclone had set the house down, very gently—for a cyclone—in the midst of a country of marvelous beauty."

It is a dramatic moment in the novel, but it doesn't compare to the scene in the film. All the scenes before that moment were shot in a monochromatic sepia. Then Dorothy opened the door and looked out on a brilliant Technicolor Munchkinland. Never, it seemed, had greens and yellows and blues and reds been more vibrantly lush. Although Technicolor had only introduced its three-color process in 1932—and first used it in a feature film in 1935—*The Wizard of Oz* and *Gone With the Wind* in 1939 convinced filmgoers around the world of its virtues. Even today the scene shocks the senses.

Shortly after Dorothy enters into the world of Munchkinland, she learns about the power structure of the Marvelous Land of Oz. It is revealed that there are four powerful witches—the Good Witches of the North and South, and the Wicked Witches of the East and West. In the MGM version of the story only three witches make an appearance, and since Dorothy's home lands on and kills the Wicked Witch of the East, just two witches have speaking roles: Glinda, the kind, wise Good Witch of the North, and the very wicked Wicked Witch of the West.

Producer Mervyn LeRoy cast Billie Burke as Glinda. In her early fifties when she took the role, Burke had enjoyed a successful Broadway career and had married Florenz Ziegfeld, the leading stage producer of the first decades of the twentieth century. They lived like royalty in their Hastings-on-Hudson estate, lavishing love on their fifteen dogs, herd of deer, lion cubs, bears, and elephant. All the while Burke continued to act—on stage, in silent films, and finally in talkies. Her specialty was the well-intentioned featherbrain. She brought this slightly ditzy quality to *The Wizard of Oz*. Dressed like a gossamer fairy, her eyes twinkling with a touch of mischief and her voice cooing like a dove, she sparkles inwardly and outwardly.

BILLY BURKE PLAYED GLINDA, THE GOOD WITCH. SHE BRINGS A LOVABLE, DITZY QUALITY TO THE ROLE.

All we know of the Wicked Witch of the East from the film is that she had excellent taste in footwear and is now dead. However, some lovers of the movie have questioned the depths of her wickedness. Famed novelist Salman Rushdie, for example, thought Munchkinland a mite "too pretty, too kempt, too sweetly sweet for a place that was, until Dorothy's arrival, under the absolute power of the evil and dictatorial Wicked Witch of the East…. [M]aybe the Wicked Witch of the East *wasn't as bad as all that*—she certainly kept the street clean, the houses painted and in good repair, and no doubt such trains as there might be, running on time. Moreover, and again unlike her sister, she seems to have ruled without the aid of soldiers, policemen or other regiments of repression." Perhaps she was a halfway decent, misunderstood Wicked Witch, akin to the Wicked Witch in the 2003 musical *Wicked: The Untold Story of the Witches of Oz.*

But there are no doubts about her sister. The Wicked Witch of the West was most thoroughly wicked, totally irredeemably wicked. To begin with—and this is not a nice thing to say—she looked like a wicked witch. The sad truth of the Marvelous Land of Oz, as Glinda explains to Dorothy, is that "only bad witches are ugly." It goes without saying that good ones are beautiful. By this ruthless standard the Wicked Witch of the West's green skin, hatchet face, pointy nose and chin, skeletal hands

MARGARET HAMILTON WAS AS WARM OFF THE SCREEN AS SHE WAS MALEVOLENT ON IT. HER CACKLING VOICE HAD THE QUALITY OF FINGERNAILS SCREECHING ACROSS A BLACKBOARD.

HAMILTON'S ROLE ENTAILED LONG SESSIONS IN THE MAKEUP
DEPARTMENT. AFTER SEVERAL WEEKS HER SKIN TOOK ON A
GREENISH HUE.

and fingers—and who knows what was beneath her singularly unattractive black hat and dress—were utterly ugly. Only in her own eyes was
she beautiful. As she shrieks at Dorothy after the young girl innocently
threw water on her, "Who'd have thought a girl like you could destroy my
beautiful wickedness." But even here her "beauty" seems more inward
than outward.

Mervyn LeRoy initially planned a very different sort of Wicked
Witch of the West. He wanted Gale Sondergaard, a thin, beautiful
brunette from Minnesota, to play the part. LeRoy had directed her in
Anthony Adverse, and she won a Best Supporting Actress Oscar for her
work. LeRoy's idea for *The Wizard of Oz* was for Sondergaard to play a
very sexy wicked witch—tight black sequined dress, sequined hat, and
makeup. Gale said, that "would be very glamorous and thus, subtly,

very wicked." But studio executives had other ideas. The children, they told LeRoy, needed "an ugly, hateful witch," and it would have taken a makeup genius to make Sondergaard ugly. She was fine with the decision. "In those days," she later said, "I was not about to make myself ugly for any motion picture."

Instead the part went to Margaret Hamilton, who in truth looked like what central casting would have sent up for the part of a witch. She

"NEVER LET THOSE RUBY SLIPPERS OFF YOU FEET OR YOU WILL BE AT THE MERCY OF THE WICKED WITCH OF THE WEST," GLINDA TELLS DOROTHY. THE BATTLE LINES ARE DRAWN, THE PRIZE REVEALED.

was a warm, sweet person, generous with her time and universally liked, but she looked like she was on the run from the Salem witch trials. If a director had a part for a New England spinster or wicked witch, she was perfect. Perfect look, perfect voice, perfect mannerism. A natural for a broom ride! So perfect, in fact, that she had already played the witch in two stage versions of *The Wizard of Oz*.

Once she was cast, wardrobe and makeup went to work, experimenting to find the best shade of green for her face and hands and the ideal witchy—but not bewitching—costume. They did their work hideously well. The sickly green makeup they applied daily on Hamilton's skin matched her marvelous screechy, menacing cackle. There were only two problems. First, the makeup smeared easily. If she touched her costume it left green streaks. When in costume she was prohibited from touching anything, making it nearly impossible to take a bathroom break or eat a meal. And when she was fed some food, she had to be careful not to ingest any of the makeup because it contained copper. Second, after several weeks of using the makeup her skin developed a greenish hue. "I suppose the stuff gradually sort of sunk into my skin,' she recalled. "It must have been months before my face was really normal again."

But she persisted, turning in a stellar performance. At the Academy Awards ceremony in the spring of 1940, Hattie McDaniel won the Best Supporting Actress Oscar for her performance in *Gone With the Wind*. That Margaret Hamilton was not nominated, let alone awarded, could only have been the result of a malevolent spell.

LIONS AND TIGERS AND BEARS

The PERFECT ENSEMBLE CAST

Try to imagine *The Wizard of Oz* with Shirley Temple as Dorothy. If there is any truth in the widely reported Hollywood rumor, it almost happened.

But as talented as she was, it is virtually impossible to imagine her as Dorothy. She would have dominated the movie with her cutesy and all-knowing little-girl charm. One can almost see her, hand on hip and bottom lip thrust outward, lecturing the Wicked Witch of the West instead of dousing her with a bucket of water. Temple could never have demonstrated the emotional range needed to capture Dorothy's character. Judy Garland displayed fear and anxiety alongside courage and good sense.

RAY BOLGER WAS A PRODUCT OF THE MUSICAL-COMEDY STAGE. HIS ROLE AS THE SCARECROW IS HIS MOST MEMORABLE.

Yet Garland's Dorothy never dominates *The Wizard of Oz*. She fits well into the ensemble. It is almost as if Dorothy, the Scarecrow, the Tin Woodman, and the Cowardly Lion form a single intelligent, caring, brave, and innocent character. Each role enhances the others.

Ray Bolger was originally cast as the Tin Woodman, but lobbied for the part of the Scarecrow, even though Mervyn LeRoy wanted Buddy Ebsen (who later found fame on *The Beverly Hillbillies*). "I'm not a tin performer," Bolger said. "I'm fluid." Eventually he got the role. A hoofer from Dorchester, Massachusetts, Bolger had worked the vaudeville circuit, acted in a few Broadway productions, and made his film debut in

The Great Ziegfeld (1936), which linked him with castmate Billie Burke (Glinda). He failed to establish a lasting Hollywood career, but *The Wizard of Oz* showcased his acting, dancing, and comedic talent. Like the other Oz-bound supplicants, Bolger's Scarecrow exudes the lost art of the vaudeville performer—telling jokes while dancing, throwing his voice as much as his body, entertaining with pantomime as broad as the Mississippi River. Yet for all the burlesque humor and pratfalls, Bolger brought a simple, irreducible humanity to the role.

The part of the Tin Woodman went to Jack Haley, another Boston-born vaudevillian. The Tin Man was rusted when Dorothy finds him and seems destined to cry himself back into the same condition for the rest of the film. Encumbered by his inflexible, bulky costume, Haley had perhaps the most difficult part to play. But he did so beautifully. "There's a great sweetness about Jack," Margaret Hamilton observed. "He did a job with the Tin Woodman that's never gotten the acclaim that it should. He was inside that armor, and it was only his eyes and his personality that made the Tin Woodman so endearing. He was so perfect for that person who wanted a heart. I believed him thoroughly. I always believed that a heart was the most important thing to Jack."

Bert Lahr's Cowardly Lion is probably the most memorable supporting character in *The Wizard of Oz*. Like Jack Haley's Tin Man, Lahr's role was an extension of his own personality. He was a nervous perfectionist, equally devoted to and obsessed with his career, fearful of failure, often unhappy off the stage but never quite at peace on it. Born Irving Lahrheim

JACK HALEY WAS A GENEROUS, SWEET MAN—THE IDEAL PERSONALITY
TO PLAY THE TIN WOODMAN. HIS HEART WAS NEVER IN DOUBT.

in New York City, he also had a successful vaudeville, burlesque, and
stage career before venturing to Hollywood, where his broad humor and
frenetic energy made him a difficult co-actor. If there was a scene to steal,
he went at it with both hands. When there was no scene to steal, he wor-
ried and fretted about his haunting inadequacies.

Yet those qualities made for a perfect Cowardly Lion. When
action, not thought, is demanded, he leaps into the fray. But given
time to think, he is apt to wring his tail, bemoan his condition, and
agonize about the future. Salman Rushdie commented that Bert Lahr's
Cowardly Lion is a "fully-realized comic masterpiece of a creation…

all elongated vowel sounds (*Put 'em uuuuuuuup*), ridiculous rhymes (*rhinoceros/imposserous*), transparent bravado and huge, operatic, tail-tugging, blubbing terror."

Of course, Judy Garland's Dorothy, a masterful innocent blank slate, allows the Scarecrow, Tin Woodman, and Cowardly Lion to have their moments of cinematic glory before they blend back into the ensemble. Shirley Temple? Imposserous!

AS THE COWARDLY LION, BERT LAHR NEARLY STOLE THE SHOW. *THE WIZARD OF OZ* SHOWCASED ALL OF HIS CONSIDERABLE TALENTS.

OF WIZARDS AND HOME

FRANK MORGAN *and the* PART *of a* LIFETIME

In Baum's novel the Wonderful Wizard of Oz appears like a perpetually campaigning politician: all things to all people. To innocent Dorothy he appears as an enormous, disembodied head with a commanding voice and a fearful aspect; to the idealistic Scarecrow he takes the form of a gossamer fairy, dressed in "green silk gauze" and wearing a crown on her "flowing green locks"; to the Tin Woodman he assumes the shape of "a most terrible beast" with the head of a rhinoceros, five eyes, and five arms; to the Cowardly Lion he is a "Ball of Fire." His shape changes and his power seems unlimited, but as the reader learns he is all smoke and mirrors, a cheap sideshow magician who was the biggest bluffer in the Marvelous Land of Oz. What proof did anyone have of his power?

His power exists because he says it does. It is true even if it isn't accurate.

Casting a wizard who was so mercurial presented challenges. Producer Mervyn LeRoy wanted Ed Wynn, known in vaudeville and on the Broadway stage as the "Perfect Fool." Harburg and assistant producer Arthur Freed hoped to get W. C. Fields. In 1938 Fields was at the height of his career, with such classics as *The Fatal Glass of Beer* (1933) and his turn in *David Copperfield* (1935) behind him and such hits as *You Can't Cheat an Honest Man* (1939) and *My Little Chickadee* (1940) just ahead. But Wynn turned the part down, as did Fields after MGM refused to agree to his contract demands. Instead the part went to Frank Morgan, a

FRANK MORGAN PLAYED THE WIZARD OF OZ. IT WAS THE ROLE OF A LIFETIME, ONE IN WHICH HE DISPLAYED HUMANITY AS WELL AS BOMBAST.

lesser actor and comedian who enjoyed a long MGM career specializing in generally well-intentioned, absentminded characters. Unlike Wynn and Fields, Morgan wanted the part, perhaps seeing it as the role of a lifetime. In his case, it was.

Virtually everyone associated with the picture liked Morgan, which was only natural because he was a consummate gentleman and true professional. He treated everyone from star to janitor kindly and never ruined a take by missing a line. All he needed was a glass of champagne or a martini now and then.

Morgan was at the center of the eeriest tale to come out of the production of *The Wizard of Oz*. According to Aljean Harmetz's delightful study of the film, the wardrobe department was looking for just the right coat for Morgan to wear in his role as Professor Marvel. They wanted something grand but seedy, a garment that a man of great pretentions but meager finances would wear. So they visited a second-hand store and purchased a rack of worn coats. With advice from Morgan and Fleming, wardrobe selected a Prince Albert coat with the velvet nap worn down to the thread. It fit Morgan and worked ideally. At one point, Morgan felt something in the pocket, and turned the pocket inside-out. Stitched inside was the name "L. Frank Baum." A bit of research confirmed that it was truly Baum's coat, and after production wrapped up it was returned to his wife. The story seems too good to be true, but several people who worked in the movie swore to it. And in Hollywood, anything is possible.

HE WAS THE INVISIBLE HAND, THE GREAT AND POWERFUL OZ, BUT
WHEN THE CURTAIN WAS PULLED BACK HE WAS REVEALED AS A
FRAUD. ONLY THE RUBY SLIPPERS AND HER CHILD'S FAITH COULD
GET DOROTHY BACK TO KANSAS.

At the end of *The Wizard of Oz*, Dorothy also makes a discovery.
After rambling around the Marvelous Land of Oz, seeing sights she never
dreamed and colors she hardly knew existed and experiencing a world
rich with adventures, she realizes that it all pales next to her Kansas home.
She tells Glinda what she has learned: "If I ever go looking for my heart's
desire again, I won't look further than my own back yard. And if it isn't
there, I never really lost it to begin with."

This theme—"There's no place like home"—touched Americans
in the late 1930s. Hollywood had always been a land of transplanted

people—Jewish immigrants from Eastern Europe, newspapermen and novelists from the East Coast and Midwest, and beautiful women and handsome men from across the country. They had all moved from their homes to chase a dream in flickering, moving pictures. They found their way to Hollywood, a place that packaged illusions. Hollywood was MGM's Technicolor Oz—beautiful, fascinating, adventurous, and packed with marvelous people. It was many things to the first generation of settlers, but it wasn't home. In this sense, *The Wizard of Oz* is the archetypal Hollywood movie.

DOROTHY INSISTS HER TIME IN OZ WAS NOT A DREAM, BUT THE MOST IMPORTANT THING IS THAT SHE IS BACK HOME.

EPILOGUE
THE LONG YELLOW BRICK ROAD

On September 18, 1949, Frank Morgan died in his sleep in his Beverly Hills home. Although he had played Professor Marvel and the Wizard in *The Wizard of Oz*, the fact was not mentioned in his long *New York Times* obituary. Most of the article focuses on his family and stage career. Only in the last paragraph is *The Wizard of Oz* mentioned, along with a list of thirty other films in which he appeared.

It seems an odd arrangement of the facts of his life. If he had died during the last fifty years, his obituary would undoubtedly have begun along the following lines: "Frank Morgan, Hollywood actor who played the Wizard in *The Wizard of Oz*, died last night in his sleep." But in 1949 *The Wizard of Oz* was not remembered as an iconic movie. Though solidly popular when it was released in 1939, it was not a box-office success. It cost $2,777,000 to make, and in its initial release grossed $3,017,000; but after MGM accounts had added in all the extras—prints, advertising, and distribution costs—the film lost money. Only on re-release in 1948–1949 did it go into the black. Back in 1939 *The Wizard of Oz* suffered from two major drawbacks. First, the millions of children who crammed into theaters with their parents to see the film paid reduced prices. And second, it had the misfortune of appearing in the same year as *Gone With the Wind*, which dominated at the box-office. *The Wizard of Oz* did nice business, attracted some warm reviews, made Judy Garland a star, and then found its way into MGM's vaults. As far as studio executives were concerned, the Yellow Brick Road was not paved with gold.

But almost two decades later *Gone With the Wind* inadvertently helped to revive the reputation of *The Wizard of Oz*. In 1956 the Columbia Broadcasting System (CBS) attempted to lease the rights to televise *Gone With the Wind* from MGM. MGM executives refused, but after several discussions with CBS a deal was worked out to broadcast *The Wizard of Oz*. CBS got the rights to two broadcasts, paying $225,000 for each one. The movie was an immediate hit, racking up staggering ratings and market shares. During the next generation the cost to broadcast the film rose. It became a yearly event for the rest of the century—a time for families to gather around their television sets and watch a revered relic of the Golden Age of Hollywood. Its characters, situations, and lines became part of American popular culture. "Follow the Yellow Brick Road." "I'll get you, my pretty, and your little dog too!" Such lines became shorthand for Americans. *The Wizard of Oz*, more than *Gone With the Wind*, became the most memorable movie of 1939.

And, of course, its legendary status has been nurtured further by spin-offs, including *The Wiz* (1978), *Return to Oz* (1985), *Wicked: The Life and Times of the Wicked Witch of the West* (1995), and *Oz: The Great and Powerful* (2013). Its appeal is as universal as coming home, as enduring as the desire to return to a simpler time and place, as timeless as innocence, heart, wisdom, and courage. It is the yellow brick road somewhere over the rainbow.

ABOUT THE AUTHOR

Randy Roberts has received two Pulitzer Prize nominations, for his books *John Wayne: American* and *Joe Louis: Hard Times Man*. He is also the author of *John Wayne Treasures* and many other books on American history. He served as a consultant for the Emmy-winning Ken Burns documentary "Unforgivable Blackness: The Rise and Fall of Jack Johnson," and has also consulted for the History Channel. Roberts is a Distinguished Professor of History at Purdue University in Indiana.